GOD WITH US, ALWAYS

Regent College 2008 Advent Reflections
Edited by Stacey Gleddiesmith

REGENT COLLEGE PUBLISHING
Vancouver, British Columbia

Published 2008 by Regent College Publishing
5800 University Boulevard, Vancouver, BC V6T 2E4 Canada
Web: www.regentpublishing.com
E-mail: info@regentpublishing.com

Regent College Publishing is an imprint of the Regent Bookstore
<www.regentbooksotre.com>. Views expressed in works published by Regent
College Publishing are those of the author and do not necessarily represent the
official position of Regent College <www.regent-college.edu>.

Library and Archives Canada Cataloguing in Publication

God With Us, Always / edited
by Stacey Gleddiesmith

ISBN 978-1-157383-430-8

1. Christmas–Meditations. 2. Advent–Meditations. I. Gleddiesmith, Stacey, 1975-

BV40.L66 2006   242'.33

CONTENTS

INCARNATION

PENTECOST

THIS PRESENT DAY

NEW JERUSALEM

GOD WITH US

Acknowledgments

This book is our third annual Advent Reader. The response of the wider Regent community to *The Cradle and the Crown* and to *Looking, Longing and Living* has been so encouraging that we dared not stop at two. I have every expectation that the blessing and refreshment our readers experienced in the first two years will be repeated.

While many in the Christian community are well aware of the brilliant writing skills of our incomparable faculty, what people have been delighted to discover these past two years is that we have a wonderful supply of talented and insightful writers among our alums. And this year has proven to be no different! To our twenty-seven writers: my deepest gratitude for accepting the invitation to write and for composing beautiful pieces that will be a blessing to many. We praise God for your giftedness and godliness.

I gratefully acknowledge the important contributions of those who made this Advent Reader possible. To Bethany Murphy, it's great to have you back as our copy editor—thank you for your careful and diligent work. Carla Faria, who does so many things for the Development office, thanks for your administrative support. There are two things I can always count on—that Dal Schindell will choose beautiful and meaningful cover art, and that Rosi Petkova, Regent's brilliant graphic artist, will give the book an attractive and professional look. Once again, I was proved right in my expectation; thank you both! And to Rob Clements of Regent Publishing, thank you for taking our work and producing this amazing book.

Our editor was advised by a team of faculty members and students in the selection of the book's theme and Scripture passages. My deepest gratitude to Bob Derrenbacker, Ross Hastings, Darrell Johnson, Ruth Chidwick and Andrew Gleddiesmith for the wonderful suggestions and feedback you gave.

There is much I could say about our editor Stacey Gleddiesmith, but I will restrict myself to this one paragraph. Here is a woman who poured her heart and soul, not to mention countless hours, into this project. The vision she had for this year's book, her capable leadership and excellent editing, have been nothing short of superb. Stacey, I am extraordinarily grateful for the way you came on board, took the reins and worked skillfully and sensitively with our diverse writers. I hope you take an extra measure of joy this Advent season in knowing that you have produced a spectacular book and a great gift for the Christian community. Thank you!

Richard Thompson
Director of Development
Regent College
Regent Alum (ThM 2000)

Introduction

S trange as it may sound, canning and the season of Advent have become linked in my mind. The process of preparing and storing summer abundance in preparation for a season of need reminds me of Mary.

Twice Mary is described as treasuring things in her heart. First, after the visit of the shepherds and their proclamation of the angel's words: "A Saviour has been born!" (Lk 2:8–20). Second, after searching Jerusalem for three days and finding twelve-year-old Jesus in the temple courts, protesting: "Didn't you know I had to be in my Father's house?" (Lk 2:41–52). Mary treasured these things in her heart. Mary took these moments and sealed them in her memory, like peaches and apricots in a jar.

Our Advent Reader is slightly different in format than it has been for the past two years. Each contributor has submitted two reflections, morning and evening, on a single passage of Scripture. Each of the very fine writers in our community who contributed to the Advent Reader this year have paid careful attention to the timing of their two reflections. They have not merely book-ended each day of Advent with the given passage—but have managed instead to enfold each day in Scripture, attentive to the way a given passage can both inform our daily tasks and allow us to rest at day's end. This enfolding is especially powerful because of our theme for this reader: The Presence of God With His People.

This year's Scripture passages have been chosen so as to walk us through the progressive revelation of God's presence: Creation, Exodus, Tabernacle, Exile, Incarnation, Pentecost, This Present Day—all leading toward the New Jerusalem, the city that is a perfect cube, the shape of the Holy of Holies where God dwells. The season of Advent is a season of long waiting. But in each historical moment of waiting, God has been drawing inexorably nearer to his people.

So in this small book, we will wait—through this very large timeline—with our God-given family. We will experience with them the ways in which God made himself present to them, the ways in which he makes himself present to us, always. For while we still wait for the fullness of God's presence, we must put things in jars. We must store up the experiences of our family. Like Mary, we must store up times when God is especially present to us, when his character is particularly clear.

In order that you might preserve these memories effectively, we invite you to read the day's Scripture in the morning, reflect on it, then read the reflections of a member of the Regent community. Each writer has a unique perspective and style of writing. They may not use the translation of Scripture with which you are familiar; enjoy the diversity of the body of Christ! When you have finished your morning reading, try to hold the thoughts prompted by this reading tucked up in the back of your mind. Let them influence how you perceive things, how you approach people, how you move through your day. Then, at the close of day, read the same passage again. Reflect on your day in light of it. Read the evening reflection provided for you. Allow consciousness of the presence of God to slip as deeply into your sleeping as it has your waking, for we have a God who neither sleeps nor slumbers.

And as you slumber, perhaps there will be the pop of a jar sealing—and that moment of clarity you had as you went about your day will be preserved: nourishment for another season. It is our hope, as you make your way through this Advent Reader, that you will feel as if *you* are being slowly and richly filled to the brim with the abundance of God's presence.

May this abundance sustain you in times of need. May it preserve you until the time when no canning is necessary: when the banquet is full.

O come, Thou Day-Spring, come and cheer
Our spirits by Thine advent here
Disperse the gloomy clouds of night
And death's dark shadows put to flight.
Rejoice! Rejoice!
Emmanuel shall come to thee, O Israel.

Stacey Gleddiesmith
Development Writer
Interim Editor of The Regent World
Regent Alum (MDiv 2007)

Genesis 1

IT IS GOOD. IT IS COSTLY.

This great chapter of beginnings is perhaps the most familiar in the Bible; it has been endlessly exegeted, explained and debated. Yet it is rarely part of our thinking about Advent.

What does this first chapter of the Old Testament have to do with the first chapters of the New? A great deal, according to John, who echoes the opening words: "In the beginning...was the word...and the word became flesh." His words pick up a theme that runs through the New Testament: that the Jesus born in Bethlehem is also "the one through whom all things were made...and in him all things hold together."

That the Incarnation was for our redemption is the urgent and obvious meaning of the Christian story. Less obvious, perhaps, is another meaning, which we are just beginning to understand: all creation is included in redemption, it's not merely a backdrop for the saving of human souls.

But the link between Christ and creation—between Advent and Genesis 1—suggests an even deeper possibility: that the Incarnation is not simply God's emergency strategy to save a spoiled creation. God has, from the beginning, chosen to share his love with a universe to whose flesh he would, "in the fullness of time," unite himself. Perhaps the Incarnation is not so much for the sake of creation, as creation for the sake of the Incarnation. This would give new meaning to the repeated phrase of Genesis: It is good.

Open, Lord, are these, thy gifts,
Gifts of love to mind and sense...

Loren E. Wilkinson
Professor, Interdisciplinary Studies and Philosophy
Regent College

4

Genesis 1

Our minds are quirky—at least mine is. I often imagine doing some wonderful creative project—then the work and risk of actually doing it create such anxiety that I block the whole business from my mind.

What if God's idea of creation had suffered the same fate? After all, creating the earth was risky: mountains could be volcanoes; snow, avalanches; seas, tsunamis; and humans could be crucifiers. Creation opens the risk of catastrophe.

Yet God is committed to such a creation, as we are reminded every Advent when we retell the story of that risky birth in a dirty, germy manger. Jesus was not born in a golden cradle covered with jewels as the early crèches would have had people believe. St. Francis changed that: *his* crèche, in a cave with live animals, is a reminder that God so loved the world that he gave his only son to enter a soiled, spoiled creation. In that birth, God, in Jesus, became lowly and poor, hungry and empty—and took on the ultimate risk of both creation and birth: death. Jesus did not die a nice tidy death on a bed surrounded by doctors, but a bloody death as his body hung by nails from a cross.

St. Francis arranged his crèche so that Mass was celebrated on the manger. The good creation was costly—for the creator; that cost, which we remember in the Eucharist, gives new life to us—and to creation.

> *Open, Lord, are these, thy gifts,*
> *Gifts of love to mind and sense;*
> *Hidden is love's agony,*
> *Love's endeavour, love's expense.*[1]

Mary Ruth Wilkinson
Sessional Lecturer
Regent College

---

[1] From W.H. Vanstone's hymn "The Risk of Love."

5

John 1:1–5

THE CREATING AND SUSTAINING LIGHT DRAWS NEAR

L ike the lens of a camera in the hands of an expert, John's "In the beginning was the Word" brings the "In the beginning, God" of Genesis 1:1 into sharp focus. The ancient portrait of the Creator now appears in its definitive form, and we discover that the agent of creation is the Word who was with God. "Without him," John boldly asserts, "was not anything made that was made."

John's insight has profound implications. The one through whom the primeval waters of the oceans and lakes were created is Christ—the Word who was from the beginning. *All things were made through him.* No wonder he could walk through the tossing waves of the sea of Galilee with majestic calm, assuring his terrified disciples as he drew near that it was he, himself, and they should have no fear. The one through whom Adam and Eve were created is Christ—the Word who was from the beginning. No wonder he could speak to the inert corpse of Lazarus in the tomb, and he who was dead came forth.

In the morning of this day, we turn our hearts in worship to adore the Word, who is God. He was there in the beginning, in that unimaginable moment outside of all time and history, poised even then to come into the world that was made through him. Nothing would be able to prevent him from drawing near.

John 1:1–5

J ohn uses light as a metaphor for life in the closing verses of our text. The essential link between the two is plainly illustrated in the realm of nature. Light from the sun energizes plants so they live, grow and produce, each after its own kind: apples and oranges, rice and corn, peas and carrots—all the gifts we must have to stay alive on this planet. There is no substitute for light; in a world deprived of it, every living thing would die.

The correspondence of light with life, the basis of John's metaphor, teaches us more about the Word who was from the beginning. It reveals that human beings can no more live apart from that Word—apart from Christ, the agent of creation through whom all things were made—than plants can live apart from the sun. To not have the light of Christ is to be exposed to the darkness, which brings death. *In him was life.*

In the evening of this day, we turn our hearts in worship to adore the Word who is God. His life is our light. By him, we are sustained and invigorated day by day. Because of him we flourish. Even in the hours of sleep, when the lamps of earth have grown dim, his light shines upon us. The darkness of this world will never be able to extinguish that light, no matter how black the darkness may seem.

Marcia Munger
Missionary Educator
Regent Alum (MCS 1975)

Acts 17:22–27

CREATED FOR RELATIONSHIP

I nherent within creation was an open communion between God and humanity; God was near.

The Creator of heaven and earth did not establish a temple relationship with his people, a relationship tied to a specific place, until after communion had been broken. The dwelling of God in the temple was meant to be a means to an end: the end being the restoration and re-creation of open communion between God and the people of God.

For almost a year now I have been trying to pull my life together as I enter the workforce day by day and seek God in weekly corporate worship. My goal has been to try to find a meaningful way to serve God, to be his hands on earth, while doing what I love.

But in my day-to-day activities, I did not find the presence of God. Frustration set in as I tried diligently to find ways to serve him with my hands. Perhaps I fooled myself, thinking that human hands are *able* to serve God. In doing so, perhaps I became more devoted to *service of* God than to *relationship with* him.

Yet in his constant grace God has gently nudged me again, reminding me through consistent time with him and through this passage that relationship, not service, is where I will experience his nearness. As you begin another day in God's presence, in what way will you foster relationship with him?

Acts 17:22–27

I s "the God who made the world and all things in it" near? Is he truly "not far from each one of us"? Uncertain, we sometimes live as if we don't know the answer to these questions. We live as if we don't remember who God is. We live like the religious Athenians: worshipping an "Unknown God."

In response to the inscription "To An Unknown God," Paul declares to the Athenians that God is near. So near, that he has appointed times and places of habitation that cause people to reach out toward him.

Yet God who is near is not only near in creation, in place and time, but also in the lives of his children. He is so near that it is "in him we live and move and exist" (v. 25). God revealed in creation is God present today in our lives. He is here with me in my habitation, and he is there with you, within the boundaries he has set for you.

As we begin this season of Advent, we await, not the "Unknown God," but the Lord of Heaven and Earth. Though the circumstances in your life may cause you to feel that God is distant and far away, take heart! For God is near. It is his very presence that causes us to seek him. It is his very presence that sustains us as we live within the boundaries of our habitation.

> *We hear the Christmas angels*
> *The great glad tidings tell;*
> *O come to us, abide with us,*
> *Our Lord Emmanuel!*

David B. Williams
Nashville, TN
System Training Manager
St. Thomas Health Services
Regent Alum (MCS 2007)

Exodus 13:17–22

"MEAGRE" BEGINNINGS OF DELIVERANCE

The world we indwell, and daily wake into, is primarily God's world of salvation and deliverance. The Israelites were burdened under the yoke of slavery in Egypt. When Christ appeared on the scene, the Roman Empire was oppressing the people of God. Sometimes the bondage goes much deeper. God's people can be in bondage to themselves: blind, deaf and hard-hearted, unwilling to receive God's way of salvation.

God delivers his people from bondage—he has done it in the past and will continue to in the future. Whether we are oppressed by political powers or by our own sin and brokenness, God calls us out of bondage and into the freedom of the life of a pilgrim. Today we are called to rise and follow him.

As pilgrims we must not forget that God's ways of deliverance are not random. They are carefully orchestrated, with consideration not only of his plan of salvation but also for our human frailty. He knows our fears and weaknesses.

Israel's journey through the desert was long and strenuous. There was no comfort of the familiar, only the hope of a promised land. So how were the Israelites, used to oppression and slavery, able to imagine a free and abundant existence in a land flowing with milk and honey? It was through the promise of God's presence. The promise that he would go before them.

Today we rise up and sing: *The Lord is my strength and song, and he has become my salvation* (Ex 15:2).

10

Exodus 13:17–22

From the outside, God's leading often seems random. Pharaoh likely thought that the Israelites were lost in the desert, wandering about without plan or aim (Ex 14:3). But when it comes to God's deliverance and guidance, first impressions aren't always accurate; in fact, they can be quite deceptive.

We see this in the way God led his people out of Egypt and into the desert (what a place!), and in the way God came to us as a babe, barely escaping the child-slaughter of King Herod. Both plans looked unpromising at first.

But in the midst of such "meagre" beginnings, God gives us a great promise: he will go before his people to lead the way, and he will deliver his people with powerful deeds. What seems at first like a hopeless situation is turned on its head—the Egyptians drown in the sea and Israel is finally free to follow their God.

With the coming of Christ, the promise of God's leading and deliverance finds its climax. Not only does God go before us to guide and deliver us, he now dwells with us in the most unlikely way: in Christ, he has become one of us so that we might be one with him.

Tonight we can rest in peace, knowing that God is with us and goes before us, in Christ. He is our great deliverer, and in him we trust.

Gisela Kreglinger
St. Andrews, Scotland
Tutor, St. Andrews University
Regent Alum (ThM 2000)

Matthew 2:13–23

LISTENING ON THE JOURNEY

The winds of tropical storm Hanna are whirring through my screened-in porch, and rain surges down my roof as I write. It is a weather crisis.

Often, in the midst of crisis, we turn to God in our need. We listen earnestly as we make our urgent requests. Crying out to God seems to be a natural reaction to tragedy, and we are more likely to listen for a response at these times. To feel he is near.

For Joseph it was different. He didn't see this crisis coming. There was no obvious threat to the safety of his family. They had just been visited by three impressive men bearing gifts, who acknowledged the baby as King of the Jews. Things were looking pretty good.

But Joseph, through his experience with an angel in a previous dream, had learned that his own perspective was sometimes limited. He listened in order to hear God's perspective. When an angel of the Lord again appeared to Joseph in a dream, he listened and knew he must take action to move his family to a place of safety, Egypt.

Joseph didn't stop listening. Later in the passage, he is told to return to the land of Israel, where he once more listens to a warning given through a dream. This leads the family to their next destination, Nazareth.

Lord,
Thank you for Joseph's listening heart.
Help me to develop this habit of listening, not only during times of crisis, but everyday,
so that I can be in the place you want me to be, doing what honours you.
Amen.

Matthew 2:13–23

As this day closes, I reflect on how well I listened. Was I able to quiet the competing voices of the world around me in order to hear the still small voice of the Master?

Joseph, recalling his journey through Egypt and back again, must have been filled with wonder. He had not known there was a threat to his family. But God knew. Like the Israelites, following God's pillar of smoke and fire into the desert, Joseph followed God's voice; and he and his family, taking one step at a time, arrived safely in Nazareth.

Often, at the end of the day, I reflect on an event or interaction that was life-giving and on an event or interaction that was difficult: the consolation and desolation of the *Ignatian Examen*. I ask God to speak to me through these life experiences.

Today, I used my GPS to navigate a new city. The direction given was a route I probably wouldn't have considered. It took me beside a crystal blue lake and between evergreen-crowned mountains; the beauty of creation was life-giving.

How like God to give an unexpected gift of joy through the unexpected source of my GPS. What unexpected joy did Israel find on their path through the barren desert? What unexpected joy did Joseph find on the road to Egypt, and the road back? What unexpected joy did God lead you into today, as you listened for his voice?

Lord, help me to listen for your voice in the unexpected events of each day.
Amen.

Julia Hindmarsh
Member of the Board of Governors
Regent College

Psalm 114

GOD'S NOMADIC DWELLING, WONDER UPON WONDER

When Israel went out from Egypt to live a nomadic life in desert tents, they became God's sanctuary, God's dominion, God's dwelling place. And they saw his glory.

Our God freed Israel from Egypt's oppression and travelled with the Israelites, leading them with mysterious columns of cloud by day and fire by night.

God took them the long way around; enemies pursued; and suddenly the sea trapped them! But Moses quieted: "Do not be afraid, stand firm and see the Lord's deliverance. He will fight for you, only keep still."

The column of cloud—the angel of God—moved to hide them, divided the sea. They crossed safely, and their splendid enemies drowned. Moses sang, "Who is like our God?" Miriam sang with the women of Israel, dancing with her tambourine: "Sing to the Lord, for he has triumphed gloriously, horse and rider he has thrown into the sea" (Ex 15:1–21).

We still sing. We still marvel, singing this psalm. The Lord did not merely *send* Israel, he went *with* them; wondrous and terrifying to their enemies, protective and comforting to his people.

When Israel lived in desert tents, they became God's dwelling place and they saw his glory. When the Christ child came, the Word became flesh and pitched his tent with *us*. He tabernacled with us. "The Word became flesh and lived among us, and we have seen his glory" (Jn 1:14).

14

Psalm 114

"They lived in a world of wonders," preached Spurgeon, "where God was seen in the wondrous bread they ate and in the water they drank, as well as in the solemn worship of his holy place."[1] Yet, in crisis, Israel forgot God's power. "Is the Lord among us or not?" asked Moses, when he named the place where water flowed from the rock (Ex 17:7). We always want assurances. In fact, we need them.

Israel was completely dependent, helpless without God's intervention. But God had made them his home, and he cared for them: he made bitter water pure, sent bread from the sky, provided water from a rock (Ex 15).

God led Israel out of Egypt by parting the Red Sea, and into the promised land by parting the Jordan. When God came near with his Word, Mount Sinai shook (Ex 19).

When the Word came near in Bethlehem, the world was again filled with wonders, and once more Israel crossed into the land of promise.

We still live in a world of wonders, although we don't always recognize this. God sometimes guides us "the roundabout way" (Ex 13:18). We encounter trouble and we panic, forgetting God's power. Detours take us places we hadn't imagined, setting us up for miracles.

We are still crossing over into wonder—with the sea parting before us. There will be singing and dancing on the other side. Look what God has done for us! Wonder upon wonder upon wonder.

Colleen Taylor
Duval, SK
Writer, Musician, Arts Steward
Regent Alum (MCS 1998)

---

[1] Charles H. Spurgeon, "The Treasury of David," *The Spurgeon Archive*, http://www.spurgeon.org/treasury/ps114.htm (accessed October 1, 2008).

15

Exodus 40:34–38

LOOKING TOWARD THE TABERNACLE

This morning, as you "tabernacle with the Lord," look around you. Observe your place of meeting and its furnishings, and reflect upon these last verses of the Book of Exodus.

The Lord has given Moses exact instructions for the building of a place to house God's presence, and it is now complete. It is a God-designed tabernacle with adornments and furnishings that are prototypes of the coming Messiah, Jesus the Saviour. The tabernacle contains a light stand (light of the world); showbread (bread of life); the Ark of the Covenant (new covenant); an altar for sacrifice (atonement); a basin for cleansing (purity); and a golden altar of incense (prayer). Each item has been methodically and symbolically put in its assigned place, and everything—including the priests who serve in the tabernacle—has been anointed and consecrated "(w)hol(l)y" to the Lord.

Think of your place of meeting with the Lord as a "tabernacle place"—whether a humble shack or a colossal mansion, a forest cathedral or a downtown condo. Wherever you are he wants to meet with you daily, by his grace, in order to bless you.

Now that everything is in its place—and you in *his* place this morning—meditate upon his word and prayerfully let the advent of his presence fill your tabernacle by his Spirit, consecrating and sanctifying you as his sacred vessel—for his use—in the day ahead.

Exodus 40:34–38

Tonight, picture yourself encamped with your fellow Israelites in the Desert of Sinai. You are in the middle of nowhere, and it has been a long day; but before closing your tent flap for the night, you take one last look above the pitched tents of your fellow travellers, toward the centre of camp and the tabernacle of the Lord.

What are you looking for? According to this passage from Exodus, you are looking for direction from the Lord: for the cloud of his presence. For whenever the cloud moved from above the tabernacle, the Israelites packed up camp and moved with it. And whenever the cloud remained, they rested.

The cloud was symbolic of God's sovereignty and lordship over his chosen people. In each hour of every day, they learned the discipline of looking continually beyond themselves to the loving God from whom they received—and expected to receive—direction, protection, provision and salvation.

With that in mind, thank the Lord tonight for his "always presence" in your life—whether awake or asleep—and expectantly look to the Lord tomorrow for his guidance and direction of your day.

As we celebrate the advent of Emmanuel, "God with us," let us continually look to the one who redeemed us and faithfully follow him to the manger, to the cross and all the way home to God's throne.

Sandra Sharpe
Washington, DC
Graphics Designer and Illustrator
Regent Alum (DipCS 1979)

2 Samuel 7:1–16

HOUSING THE PRESENCE OF GOD

In yesterday's reading, the glory of the LORD filled the tabernacle. A small tent-like structure enclosing the "Ark of the Covenant," the portable tabernacle was the visible symbol of Divine Presence. The inaccessibility of the Ark, hidden as it was in the "Holy of Holies," heightened the sense of awe connected with the Glorious Presence (the "Shekinah"). It was abundantly clear that where the Ark was, there was Yahweh. The nation was *defined* by this Presence.

With Israel's settlement in Palestine comes a new challenge. A nation of nomads, leaving their tents behind, begins to build houses. An idealized "land of promise" becomes a realized homeland. As the narrative unfolds, a measure of political and military stability seems within reach, focused on the divine choice of the legendary shepherd-king, David.

As 2 Samuel 7 opens, we find David securely ensconced in Jerusalem, in a cedarwood palace replete with the Ancient Near Eastern comforts befitting a successful monarch. But where, in all of this, is "the Presence?" At this point David conceives a brilliant idea. Why not build Yahweh, formerly as nomadic as the nation itself, his own house? The Presence must be given permanence.

But can a *human being* give God permanence?

Perhaps this desire to tie God to a place lies behind our own nostalgic desire to hold on to "the Christmas Spirit" all year. We want to build structures, to hang on to holy moments. If only we could build a permanent manger.

Holy God, forgive us when we try to tie you down.
Help us to better understand your Presence.

18

2 Samuel 7:1–16

What was God's answer to David's suggestion? After a night's sleep, David's court-prophet Nathan returns with a divine word. Simply translated, it says, "Would you build me a house to live in?" followed by Yahweh's reminder that in all of his nomadic years with Israel, he never asked, "Why have you not built me a house of cedar?"

A great reversal follows. The divine word is clear: David, it's not about *you* building *me* a house, but about *me* building *you* a house. You and the people I have chosen are my real house. I will plant you and establish you and make your kingdom eternal. I will even raise up one of your sons who will "build a house for my name," but more to the point, I will never abandon my promise or withdraw my presence. In short, I AM "God with You." Now. Always.

Christmas is about the fulfilment of that promise and the arrival of that Presence. What we call the "Davidic Covenant" was established for David's time and ours; God's own king was coming. To God's unconditional grace given to Abraham was added God's unconditional presence through a descendent of David.

David wanted to build a temple, so the Glorious Presence would always be there, right next to his own palace. But, in Yahweh's kingdom, that isn't how it works. We don't bring God into our plans, settling him where we will. No, he comes and dwells among us on his terms. We are his house; he is "Emmanuel, God with Us."

Carl E. Armerding
Former Professor and President
Regent College

Matthew 1:18–25

BRINGING JOSEPH INTO THE PICTURE

We quickly recognize Annunciation scenes: there is the demure Mary in a posture of devotion—usually reading a book, bless her heart. And there is the powerful angel, harbinger of troubling and momentous news, prologue to the mighty overshadowing of the Spirit by which the Christ will be conceived. The dynamic of the visual or literary representation is a duet between two figures.

But in historic fact, it was a trio—or at least a set of duets. There is Joseph to consider. Matthew's account, emphasizing as it does Jesus' patrilineal descent, shows us what the artists and the poets often do not: the way in which Joseph is brought into the picture.

His angel is once-removed, mediated through a dream—both less tangible and more mysterious than Mary's announcer. But the message interlocks perfectly, like two puzzle pieces, with the one that Mary has received and repeated to Joseph. As "acting father," Joseph is given the privilege of naming the child. As husband, he is given assurance of Mary's fidelity and purity. As believer, he is given word of the divine nature and human-divine origin of The Child who is about to take over Joseph's life.

Joseph, a man willing to lay down his life for a child not of his own begetting, is the saint of every friend, every adoptive parent, every teacher, every pastor who takes another's child into their hearts. He is the saint of ordinary people caught up in the extraordinary purposes of God to love and to save the world.

Matthew 1:18–25

As though a dream-mediated angelic announcement might not be sufficiently convincing for some readers, Matthew's account adds the first of what will be eleven "this-took-place-to-fulfill" cross-references in his gospel. Like an underlined hypertext link, each of these references draws the contemporary narrative into alignment with the Great Story of God's fulfilling his promises to Abraham.

As I have pondered this passage, I have wondered at what point the reference to Isaiah 6:5 became part of the story. Was it a later interpolation? Did the tradition of finding Old Testament passages related to events in Jesus' life originate in Jesus' own private explanations of "what was said in all the Scriptures concerning himself" (e.g., Lk 24:25–27)? Or is there just the hint of a chance that, as Mary went to consult with her older cousin, Elizabeth, so Joseph might have sat down with his aged relative, Zacharias.

Perhaps the silenced Zacharias opened a scroll and showed Joseph the words that satisfied him at last: beyond the dream-message, a more sure word. Perhaps Zacharias wrote, with an aged, arthritis-warped finger on a dusty table, the Hebrew letters of the Scripture reference; and Joseph, with his synagogue training, knew instantly that *this* event that was reshaping his own life and his view of reality was *that* event foretold by the prophets.

Now Joseph has a second name for his son-to-be-born, the most precious name of them all: Emmanuel. This Jesus-Saviour will bring God's presence to his people because he *is* God's presence. God with us. Then. And now.

Maxine Hancock
Professor, Interdisciplinary Studies and Spiritual Theology
Regent College

Isaiah 7:1–17

WILFUL EXILE OR WILLING RECIPIENT

S igns are meant for our good. Be it a "One Way" or a "No U-Turn" sign, we ignore them at our peril. When lost or confused, we desperately look for signs to guide us—the larger and clearer, the better.

Ahaz is offered a sign—any sign he wants—a sign from God. A demonstration of God's promised presence. But Ahaz does not want a sign. Although invited, he will not ask. Apparently he does not want to hear any confirmations of God's faithfulness.

It sounds crazy: to rely on ourselves rather than the God who made us and loves us; to refuse a sign from God when it is clearly offered. And yet, maybe not so crazy. Perhaps Ahaz knows what we know—that there is no half-way with God. Perhaps he knows that God will demand other changes: an overhaul of his economic choices, a cleansing of the sexual practices he accepts and repentance for the way he stewards his resources of power. Ahaz, like us, is wilfully unprepared for a renovation of the heart.

Wilfulness is equivalent to exile. It is the internal "NO!" that kills relationship. Wilfulness makes "*God with us*" a sign of judgment. All too often, we allow this stubborn wilfulness to creep into our own lives.

As you go about your day, consider this question: Where *don't* I want the kingdom of God to overrule the kingdom I have built for myself?

Lord, forgive me for the ways I have been unresponsive and closed to you.
Give me the grace to willingly receive your Living Presence.

Isaiah 7:1–17

I n the gap left by Ahaz's unresponsiveness, God provides his own response—an unexpected and strange response—*a girl with child.*

Classic English has an interesting way of describing a pregnant woman: "She *fell* pregnant." Pregnancy "comes upon" the woman. This contrasts the oft-used expression, "She *got* pregnant," which nicely parallels other things we "get"—like cars or computers or cameras. Perhaps the first phrase is more accurate: fruitfulness is not something we "get" or even "are," it is always something we *receive*, something that falls upon us by grace.

In this Old Testament precursor to the advent of our Lord, we may not have Mary's *"let it be to me as you have said,"* but we do have a girl with child as the sign of God's presence. We have a living sign—embodied—showing all who have eyes to see the kind of posture God desires, no, *requires* of us, if we are to be a people who can welcome the advent of his presence with open arms and open hearts.

The opposite of the *wilfulness* that kills (and exiles) is the *willingness* that receives. It is willingness that God seeks. It is willingness that seeks God.

Looking back on the day that has just passed, for which moments can you give thanks that you prayerfully and willingly waited on God? When were you wilfully carrying on with your own agenda? What prayer does the answer to these two questions call forth from you?

Geordie Ziegler
PhD Candidate in Systematic Theology
University of Aberdeen
Regent Alum (MDiv 1998)

Jeremiah 7:1–29

A CONDITIONAL CHRISTMAS, A PROMISE OF PRESENCE

Life is cyclical. We go from sunrise to sunset and back to sunrise again; from Sunday to Saturday and back to Sunday again; from Christmas to Easter and back to Christmas again. The cycles of life give comfort and security. We rarely question the dependability of these daily, weekly and annual cycles. The cyclical character of time assures us that it will be Christmas by the time we have come to the end of our Advent Reader.

Jeremiah, however, is not a prophet of cycles. He interrupts the regularity of time. In the sharpest way possible, he removes our comfort and security. Jeremiah is the prophet of the great "IF." Interrupting our confidence that Christmas will come around this year like it did the previous year, he cautions us sharply: "IF you really change your ways and your actions...IF you do not oppress the alien, the fatherless or the widow...THEN I [the Lord] will live in this place with you" (7:5–7, my translation). God will live in this place—Christmas will come around—IF we act justly.

We tend to avoid Jeremiah, because with Jeremiah even Christmas, our favourite time of year, seems no longer secure. In reality, however, it is our sinful avoidance of the prophetic denunciation, not the gracious prophetic condition, which ruptures the cycle of life and prevents Christ from entering into our hearts. By letting Jeremiah's condition give shape to our lives, we allow Advent to lead into Christmas.

O holy Child of Bethlehem,
Descend to us, we pray.
Cast out our sin, and enter in,
Be born in us today.

Jeremiah 7:1–29

God's promises often seem fragile to us, and this chapter fuels our anxieties. At a time in which Judah's national survival is in serious doubt, Jeremiah offers chastisement rather than comfort: "Do not trust in deceptive words and say, 'This is the temple of the LORD, the temple of the LORD, the temple of the LORD!'" (7:4). The sharp indictment ends with God saying he has "rejected and abandoned" the people of Judah (7:29). How can we trust, then, in God's faithfulness?

We cannot undo this chapter's divine threat of exilic abandonment. But the threat does not stand alone. The threat of abandonment is preceded by a promise of presence. Three times, Jeremiah insists that the temple bears God's Name (vv. 10, 11, 14), reminding us of Deuteronomy's ancient promise that God would live in his temple (Dt 12). At the very moment that we are tempted to give up on God's integrity, we are reminded that he has promised his presence to a particular place.

Not only is the threat of abandonment *preceded* by a promise of presence; it is also *followed* by one. This passage is another Advent passage. Jesus is the new Temple, whose Name is above every Name (Phil 2:9). God's promise of presence outshines his threat of abandonment. Our greatest fears about the integrity of God yield in the presence of the promise of Christmas.

O come, O come, Emmanuel,
And ransom captive Israel,
That mourns in lonely exile here
Until the Son of God appear.

Hans Boersma
J. I. Packer Professor of Theology
Regent College

Matthew 1:1–17

EXPOSED LIVES

We come to Advent eager and sincere, but sometimes feeling too travel-weary to prepare, to make ourselves ready in the way we think we ought. But perhaps all we need is just enough emptiness within to receive God's gift. Maybe all God is looking for is the smallest of openings, a crack of desire, enough space within which to rediscover that we are as passionately loved as we are desperately in need of rescue.

Between the commas and repetitive phrases of Matthew's genealogy lurks a whole community of fellow pilgrims, layered windows into desire and quandary. Abraham, with his promise that survives the reign of the kings, good and bad, and the exile in Babylon. King David's consuming devotion to God and his wrenchingly misspent passion, unavoidably witnessed to by this marvelously puzzling jewel: "And David was the father of Solomon by the wife of Uriah..." Puzzling because when Solomon was born, Bathsheba, the wife of Uriah, was lawfully David's wife.

Uriah was a Hittite, a loyal servant who was betrayed by David's adultery, then murdered to cover it up. Hundreds of years later, his name and his story are remembered in the genealogy of God's long-awaited Messiah, reminding us of the God to whom each one matters, by whom no name is overlooked, no circumstance forgotten. Then, in the latter third of the genealogy, apart from two names, the rest are unknown generations, waiting in exile, known only to God.

In what exile or silence do we find ourselves now, and how are we remembered?

Matthew 1:1–17

The mention of Joseph breaks the pattern of the other males cited. He is not a father, but the husband of Mary. Mary's name is added to the list of women who committed ethically questionable acts, or were non-Israelites but took passionate risks and became heroines of Jewish piety. We are called to be a holy people, and yet Jesus' lineage is full of hypocrisy, sacrilege, sexual scandal and confusion.

And what about us? How did we enter God's story? By whose spirit or blood-lines have we come?

As tedious as Matthew's litany of names may be, it's the perfect place to begin the story of the genesis of Jesus, God's Christ. This representative list, this panorama of exposed lives through story-upon-story, makes it possible for us to believe that, just maybe, the broken language of our own lives is also part of God's ongoing story in the world. This list can help us believe that to live passionately is essential, and that our need to be rescued from misspent passion is why we journey.

But thanks be to God, we do not journey alone. To accompany us, we have the stories of our lives, the blessed Trinity and the community of faith—in this place and elsewhere. We are all wanted in God's story; we all belong to God's story. May we be graced to have a glimpse of our place within it as we entrust our lives to God in rest.

> *...the long work*
> *of turning their lives*
> *into a celebration*
> *is not easy. Come...*[1]

Diane S. George Ayer
Calgary, Alberta
Circulation Supervisor, Ambrose University College Library
Regent College (1980–1984)

---

[1] Mary Oliver, "The Sunflowers," in *New and Selected Poems* (Boston: Beacon Press, 1992), 138–139.

Luke 1:26–38

BREAKING INTO TIME AND PLACE

Angels and babies. Luke's opening chapter gives us angels and babies as signs of God's presence among us. Taken no further, we can easily associate these with our cultural images of the Christmas season. Cherubs—plump, benign and curly-haired—adorn our decorations and cover our greeting cards. Part angel, part baby, they gild our world, announcing...what?

Luke's angels and babies can't be packaged as cherubs. The breaking-in of God's kingdom in this text is anything but mild and unobtrusive. It cannot be relegated to a pretty backdrop.

Gabriel is sent to announce God's incarnate presence in history. Gabriel, who speaks with authority, who stands in the throne room of God, is the angel sent to the households of Zechariah and Mary. We are not told exactly what Gabriel looks like, but surely he is more like a soldier than a plump child. He brings news of the advance of God's kingdom; good news that is strangely tied up with the cooperation of the weak for its flourishing. There is no sentimentality here.

No, there is an intrusion, a take-over, a choosing of sides. God will not appear to us as a bright light or as a glowing angel who grants our wishes. God will change the entire order of creation on our behalf. He will not leave the world as he found it. He will not merely improve it. He will overcome it. And that overcoming starts here, with angels and babies. May we see them as they are.

Luke 1:26–38

This passage in Luke is so familiar, and yet so extraordinary. It reads like a news report, loaded with specific concrete details related to the event at hand. It is the sixth month of Elizabeth's pregnancy; Gabriel is sent to Galilee; and Mary is a virgin rooted in time and space.

Imposed on this physicality of creation is a word, *the* Word, which was in the beginning, is now and forever shall be. "How will this be?" Mary asks.

Matter-of-factly, the angel answers: the Holy Spirit will come upon Mary, and so God will take part in the physical world in a new way. *Matter, in fact,* comes into being from the spoken Word of God, from the Holy Spirit's covering, from the power of He who ordered the universe. Nothing is impossible for God.

Stunning.

Yet, we have become comfortable with this description of God's breaking-in, this physical presence of God among us, as one of us. We read the text like *yesterday's* paper. Factual. True. A little strange, but distant in time and place.

God's kingdom breaks in, factually, truly, strangely. But not distantly. It is here—in this time and place, too. It grew from the formation of a prophet in Elizabeth's womb to God's own Son, born of a virgin. It grew from a small town in Galilee to a cross in Jerusalem, to the ends of the earth. The Kingdom of God is here, and its presence is more real than the evening news.

Jennie McLaurin
Dean of Students and Associate Professor of Bioethics
Regent College
Regent Alum (MCS 2007)

Luke 1:39–45

WAITING TOGETHER, REJOICING TOGETHER

Waiting is not easy for any of us. Waiting with hope for good news is hard when much of the news we hear is bleak and dark. It is especially difficult to wait with trusting expectation if we are isolated from other hopeful people.

What was it like for Elizabeth and Mary to be women in waiting? In a harsh, oppressive world in which those in power held an iron fist over those who barely scraped by, these two women waited for the reality of the impossible to come to birth, literally. Both carried a sign within their wombs that God was not silent, distant or uncaring.

The God of Abraham and Isaac, who spoke through the prophets Isaiah and Micah, was on the move, preparing God's people for the coming of his presence—in such a way that the world would never be the same.

How do you wait in such a pregnant moment? How is it possible to hold onto hope inside yourself when the surrounding world is cynical and ominous?

Mary "went with haste" seventy miles to the side of her pregnant cousin Elizabeth to gain support, and to hope in community. Elizabeth embraced Mary as the baby John leaped inside of her with joy. Together they helped one another be women of hope, believing that what the Lord had spoken was true.

With whom is Jesus inviting you to wait, trusting that the word he has spoken is true?

Luke 1:39–45

In Romans 12:15, we are invited to "rejoice with those who rejoice; mourn with those who mourn." I've found rejoicing to be the harder task. When faced with another person's success, jealousy sneaks in, squeezing out our desire to celebrate another person's accomplishments. Instead of rejoicing in how God is choosing to uniquely work through another individual, our own need for praise consumes us.

Elizabeth's example provides us with hope of another way to respond—a Spirit-filled way to respond. When her younger cousin arrived eagerly at her doorstep, Elizabeth knew that the child growing inside of Mary would be greater than the longed-for boy kicking inside of her. Did she also know that it would be Mary who would be revered and of whom songs would be sung?

Mary came in need of support from her older, more experienced cousin, and Elizabeth responded—not out of selfishness or jealousy—but as one who listens to the Spirit. As the baby John leaped for joy inside her, Elizabeth was able to celebrate God's big story of salvation and speak the words of affirmation that the mother of her Lord needed to hear: "blessed are you among women."

Elizabeth reminds us that when we rejoice with those who rejoice, we are celebrating a God intimately involved in history and in the lives of people. There would come a time of mourning for both mothers; but at this time, Elizabeth was called to celebrate the babe in Mary's womb, the Saviour of the world.

Let us, too, rejoice!

Renée Notkin
Seattle, WA
Worship and Spiritual Formation Pastor, Union Church
Regent Alum (MDiv 1991)

Luke 1:46–56

OUR SONG OF HUMILITY

L uke's detailed account of the Incarnation includes Mary's beautiful song of praise on the occasion of her visit to Elizabeth. As you read Luke 1:46–56, consider that in Mary's Magnificat we hear the very first hymn of the Christian era.

Like all devout Israel, Mary had been awaiting the coming of Messiah. Astonishingly, the moment of salvation arrives, and she *herself* carries the divine promise in her womb. In Jesus, God is now physically dwelling amidst his people.

When Elizabeth recognizes Mary as "the mother of my Lord," Mary's heart pours out this joyous, Scripture-imbued song of exaltation to the Mighty One.

Her song is *our* song. The Virgin Mary is the first to bear Christ—Jesus is uniquely alive within her. But what she experiences physically, we are destined to share with her spiritually. "If, according to the flesh the Mother of Christ is one alone," says St. Ambrose, "according to the faith all souls bring forth Christ." Mary's singular experience renders her the proto-Church, the first of many who carry Jesus within them.

Mary's song is thus the initial moment of worship in the new order of faith. Anticipating the salvation effected by the Son she is carrying, Mary, on her own behalf and on behalf of all who will trust in Christ, lifts to God a splendid hymn of humble gratitude extolling the Lord's mighty acts, filled with wonder that he has made himself one with us.

Luke 1:46–56

I f anyone ever had grounds for self-congratulation, it was Mary, the "favoured woman" chosen to facilitate the Incarnation of her Creator. But God selected her with infinite wisdom. Mary's *fiat*, her unreserved "yes" to God, locates her among Israel's eminent exemplars of faith; yet she declines to grasp at the inestimable glory attending the event. Mary knows that this spectacular act is attributable solely to Almighty God.

Mary's humility in Luke 1:46–56 beautifully echoes the meekness of Christ, who "did not regard equality with God as something to be exploited" (Phil 2:8), and who "came not to be served but to serve others" (Mk 10:45). Mary understands her role is sheer gift; accordingly, her hymn focuses on God's mighty deeds among his people.

In the life of faith, humility is inextricably linked with service. Luke 1:56 underscores Mary's humble words with concrete deeds. She who bears the Messiah awaits his birth while providing three months of caring assistance to her much older cousin Elizabeth, helping to bring John the Baptist into the world. In Mary's own wondrous moment of blessing, she demonstrates her heart's genuinely humble disposition by rendering service to another, further verifying her declaration in 1:38, "I am the Lord's servant."

For centuries, the Church has incorporated Mary's *Magnificat* into its liturgical life; in the West, it appears at Vespers—Evening Prayer. Thematically, Mary's song exhibits the only deportment appropriate in the presence of God: dependent humility. It is fitting that we pray it while surrendering ourselves to his care at day's end.

Roland Carelse-Borzel
Vancouver, BC
Director of Admissions, Regent College (2000–2004)
Regent Alum (MCS 1999)

Matthew 3:1–12

RADICAL PREPARATION, DRENCHED WITH THE SPIRIT

The enigmatic John the baptizer was no mere footnote to the story of Jesus. He was an introduction. And a challenging one at that! His appearance was strange and his language both invitational and confrontational. He went about the task of preparation for the coming of the long-awaited one like a bull in a china shop. There was nothing gentle about this man.

In our "soft" culture and equally pampered Western Christianity where all is about comfort and little about challenge, let alone transformation, John would likely not get an invite to many of our parties or events. He is just too "in your face."

Yet John is God's chosen servant to prepare the way for the mission of Jesus. God's way, it seems, is not about niceties, but about radical preparation. Life shattering preparation! A preparation not simply of submission to external rituals, such as baptism, but a change of values rooted in deep repentance.

In this Advent season, as we again anticipate the coming of the one who alone gives salvation and life to the world, and as we prepare ourselves for his presence amongst us, let us be open to being shaken and confronted.

Let us move ourselves from the willing crowds seeking baptism and place ourselves in the company of the double-minded Pharisees and Sadducees. And in that place, allow ourselves to become candidates for a more radical preparation for the coming of Jesus—a preparation not simply of inward piety, but of life-style transformation.

Matthew 3:1–12

John the baptizer, God's "severe" messenger, is not the whole story. He is the introduction to the story of Jesus, and in that introduction lies the jewel of a promise. A promise that points to so much more than the hard work of inner confrontation, repentance and outer transformation. This jewel is the promised comforter, the Holy Spirit, the energy of God, the third person of the Trinity.

John thus not only points us to Christ, the lamb of God who takes away the sins of the world, but also to the gift of the Spirit that Jesus will bestow.

This gift of the Spirit is no little impartation. It is not a mere add-on. The Spirit is going to be bucketed over us. We will be drenched. Immersed. Saturated. In this gift lies the promise that the work of renewal is not simply our work. It is not our self-effort. It is what God will do.

Advent is the season of anticipation. We wait for the One coming toward us. And this long-awaited one comes laden with gifts—the most surprising of which is the Spirit who comes to dwell with us, purify us and carry us forward. Advent and Pentecost belong together. And in the gift of the Spirit lies the hope of inspiration, energy, sustenance and renewal.

In the love of God, the grace of Christ and in the upward wing of the Spirit, we live in love, joy and service.

Charles R. Ringma
Professor Emeritus, Mission and Evangelism
Regent College

Acts 2:1–4, 36–39

RESPONDING TO THE SUDDEN-BUT-NOT-UNEXPECTED

In Acts 2, Luke tells us what happened as the first followers of Jesus were in that cramped upper room at Pentecost. They were "all together in one place," awaiting what had been promised down through history. Suddenly, this group was empowered as a community of believers, but each with individual gifts. They were empowered and equipped to proclaim the good news that Jesus of Nazareth is the crucified and resurrected Messiah.

The events of Pentecost were sudden, but not unexpected. Not only did the prophet Joel predict this event, John the Baptist also anticipated a baptism "with the Holy Spirit and fire" (Lk 3:16). Even Jesus himself foresaw Pentecost, telling his disciples to stay in Jerusalem until they had been "clothed with power from on high" (Lk 24:49).

Like Pentecost, the advent of our Lord Jesus is a sudden, but not unexpected, event. And like the first followers of Jesus at Pentecost, during Advent we are called to gather together as a community of believers to await the sudden-but-not-unexpected in-breaking of the divine realm into the human. Like Pentecost, the Incarnation equips us, together as a community of believers, to proclaim the Good News of Jesus the Messiah.

During this season of Advent, as we await the sudden-but-not-unexpected coming of our Lord Jesus Christ, let us ponder how God has gifted us as individuals to work with the community of the fellow faithful to proclaim the good news that Jesus of Nazareth has come as our Messiah.

Acts 2:1–4, 36–39

We see in our reading that the special manifestation of God's Holy Spirit in the upper room of Acts 2 was the realization of a long-promised appearance of God's presence. The latter part of Acts 2 describes how many people responded to this sudden-but-not-unexpected Holy Spirit empowerment and Peter's subsequent exposition of it.

We see in particular how many Jews living in Jerusalem responded to Pentecost—Luke tells us that they were "cut to the heart" (Acts 2:37). Because of their response, Peter tells these new disciples to repent, be baptized and expect to receive the gift of the Holy Spirit.

What does it mean to be "cut to the heart"? We see a similar expression in Psalm 109:22, connoting a sense of sharp conviction, remorse and neediness. Peter tells these new converts to "repent" upon witnessing Pentecost, so that they too might experience the manifestation of God's Holy Spirit.

Advent is recognized as a penitential season in the Church's calendar. Repentance is a regular and frequent part of this season of preparation, as we once again prepare to welcome Jesus the Messiah in our midst. During Advent, as at Pentecost, repentance allows us to experience God's in-breaking to human affairs and history.

During this season of Advent, may we ponder those darker corners of our lives in need of some light. For it is in repenting of our sin that we are able to allow Jesus to be born again in our midst.

Robert Derrenbacker
Assistant Professor of New Testament Studies
Regent College

Ezekiel 36:24-35

ROCK GARDENS

W hat a picture Ezekiel paints for us: our barren heart of stone transformed into a heart of flesh...the Spirit within us, moving us into life
and fruitfulness.

Ezekiel was called to be a prophet while in Babylon. His mandate was to prepare the people of God for imminent destruction and ultimate resurrection: Jerusalem razed and restored. If Israel would not be the people of God, God would
send his Spirit to *make*, for himself, a people. The forceful God-with-us who speaks
through Ezekiel stands in sharp contrast to the popular image of the babe in the
manger—that peaceful picture of God's unassuming presence among us.

Sometimes, God is *loudly* present. I confess, in those times I find myself wish-
ing for a "still, small voice." The God of warm, fuzzy love is more comfortable,
especially when I am curled up within my own heart of stone, favourite idols
clutched close.

Instead, I get what I need—a violent upheaval: a volcanic eruption on the job,
a landslide of family pressures, a flood of financial concerns. A razing of my false
gods of security. God loudly with me.

In the Pacific Northwest, we are familiar with the sudden frosts that freeze
rivulets of rain—fingers of icy fissures that blast through solid rock. In the course
of seasons, the rain and wind loosen rocky cliff sides and fields of stone become
muddy and messy, then infused with roots and vegetation. In spring, stone finally
yields to drifts of grasses, fireweed, elderberry and wild rose. Beauty rises from
ashes, joy from crisis, life from stone.

Ezekiel 36:24–35

"**I** will remove your heart of stone and give you a heart of flesh... You will be my people and I will be your God" (vv. 26, 28). Talk about soaring on eagle's wings! Briefly. "I want you to know that I am not doing this for your sake...Be ashamed and disgraced for your conduct, O house of Israel" (v. 32). What a way to kill a great promise!

Before we can draw ourselves fully erect, looking nobly into the horizon, pondering our lofty heritage, the focus is shifted. We learn that the transformation of our heart of stone into a heart of flesh has unimagined consequences: we will be able to feel how disgustingly we have behaved.

Stone doesn't feel much. Can a stone weep? Can it repent? Flesh, on the other hand, is intimate with pain, regret and self-loathing.

But perhaps our pain is our touchstone, the acknowledgment of our true heritage: that we have been transformed, endowed with hearts of passion capable of resilience, grief and great joy. It is authentic living, in the midst of chaos, heart-grief, loneliness and desolation; it is our flesh and blood and tears, not the secure tranquility of stone, that reveals our true birthright and mandate: "You will be my people."

God has declared us his own people. This is *his* work—transforming stone into a garden. God's utterly creative re-creation of our hearts through his Spirit, cannot fail.

They will say, "This land that was laid waste has become like the garden of Eden" (v. 35).

Faith Richardson
Langley, BC
Nursing Faculty, Trinity Western University
Regent Alum (MCS 1997)

Titus 2:11–14

THE SILENT MEASURE

You and I inhabit a time in history that is defined by its context, by what has preceded and by what will follow. We live suspended, as it were, between Christ's first and second advents. An amazing space.

This reminds me of another breathtaking space which is also defined by its context. Each time we hear the "Hallelujah Chorus" in Handel's *Messiah*, we are suspended in the silent measure, filled with wonder as the tiny pause, conspicuously void of all sound, washes over us. We wait and can hardly bear the suspense until the final "Hallelujah!" breaks through the silence, leaving our hearts and eyes full.

But what of the silence? Is the silent measure only a vacuum, defined by the absence of notes? Ah, therein lies the beauty. Much more than the absence of sound, it is imbued with wonder and meaning because of its context. The space takes our breath away *because* of what has preceded and what will follow. Within the space itself, nothing is happening, and everything is happening.

As you walk through this particular day, I encourage you to ponder the notion of waiting. Wherever you find yourself, in whatever circumstance of waiting, I encourage you to dwell richly in that space. God is in it with you this day. May your silent spaces be filled with beauty and meaning.

Titus 2:11–14

As one whose vocation is, in part, to provide a place of rest and prayer for others, I have the opportunity to see the transformation of individuals while they are still. Most who arrive tired and discouraged later leave refreshed and strengthened. Nothing is happening, and everything is happening, in their stillness.

However, quiet waiting does not come easily to most of us. As Frederick Buechner writes, "We are none of us very good at silence. It says too much."[1]

You and I wait for both the heavenly and the earthly; and the earthly waiting, accompanied by heartache, can bear down on us. As we wait for our Lord's return, our earthly concerns live side-by-side with our heavenly hope.

For what or for whom do you wait? Perhaps you have yet to make request of the Father. Perhaps you have already asked him, and now...you...wait. Between the time you make the request and the time you begin to see his answer, you inhabit yet another amazing space—a silent measure. Nothing is happening, while everything is happening.

Beloved, the Father has heard your request. He gives to you in the waiting, and even as you sleep (Ps 127:2). He is in this space with you, and his hand is on you and yours. One day the silent waiting will be broken with the "Hallelujah!" In the meantime, drink deeply.

"The Lord is in his holy temple; let all the earth be silent before him."
Habakkuk 2:20

Rebecca B. Conti
Flagstaff, Arizona
Speaker and Minister, Hidden Hollow Prayer Retreat
Regent Alum (MCS 2004)

---

[1] Frederick Buechner, *Listening to Your Life* (New York: Harper, 1992), 284.

Galatians 3:23–4:7

CLOTHED WITH THE SPIRIT OF HIS SON

As children sometimes doubt whether they belong to their family, so many of the gentile Galatians doubted their true inclusion in the family of God. And what do insecure children do? Anything to fit in. So Paul, angry and impassioned, assures them of their unique identity, an identity not defined by the law. He confesses to them, *At one time we Jews were like a son who had not yet come of age—we had to obey our tutor, the law, at all times. But a time was coming when we would become mature.*

Then he turns to them and extends the metaphor: *You also are sons.*

Hear the strange particularity of Paul's metaphor here:

You are a son, Paul says to the outcast gentile.

You are a son, Paul says to the orphaned slave.

You are a son, Paul says to the penniless woman.

Not a *child,* but a *son.* And if a son, then an heir.

The world has always found identity in ethnicity, class and gender. And so the world has always been waiting for the advent of One who could robe all differences with his glorious status.

And you Galatians have reached your arms out like a child waiting to be dressed. But the age of maturity is now. The time has come for you yourself to *put on* Christ, to become a son because you clothe yourself in the robe of the Son. As C. S. Lewis noted, we are not most ourselves when stripped bare, but when fully clothed.[1]

---

[1] C.S. Lewis, *The Four Loves* (San Diego: Harcourt Brace Jovanovich, 1960), 147.

Galatians 3:23–4:7

During my first year in Vancouver, far from home, I learned two important lessons. The first was that mountains are rain-makers. Unfortunately, in the many rainy nights that ensued, I experienced severe depression and began to doubt God's love. Still, in this desert of feeling one strong longing surfaced, the longing for a father.

In deserts, we forget the lush evidences of God's presence. Forgetting the many times God had drawn near to me, I doubted having ever received God's Spirit. And the father-cry of my heart clambered louder. In this mood, one night, I turned to Galatians and read, *Because you are sons, God sent forth his Spirit into our hearts, crying out, "Abba, Father."*

Reading these words, I realized that the Spirit *was* present in my heart—in the cry of *Father*. A cry not just of longing, but—I then recognized—also of confidence. Paul says this is how you experience God's presence now, even in deserts: the Spirit cries from within you with the intimate language of the Son. *Abba*—the name only Jesus spoke. A name of trust. A tender name used as a little child but still spoken as an adult son.

This, then, was the second lesson I learned that first rainy year: by the Spirit, we inherit not only a new status, but also a new relationship. We experience God's presence now every time we cry "Father." And in time, our Father promises, it will rain not only in the mountains, but in the desert as well.

Our Father in Heaven. Come.

Mary Romero
Poet and Literature Teacher
Regent Alum (MCS 2008)

Revelation 12

IN THE PRESENCE OF THE ENEMY

S ad it is at Christmastime to consider poor Mary giving birth in a stable. In the nightmare of Revelation 12, however, this great mother—blessed by heaven (sun and moon) and representing Israel (twelve stars)—must do God's will and give birth *in the presence of her enemy*, that old dragon who has bedevilled every child of our first mother, Eve.

We tend to fear banks and insurance companies and credit card issuers because we want money and they may or may not give it to us. We tend to fear physicians and dentists and hospitals because we want health and they represent our loss of it, even as they try to help us regain it. We tend to fear news of global climate change because we want stability and comfort while the weather threatens us with chaos and disaster.

These fears make sense. But we must not forget to fear the dragon. For he prowls about, seeking our very life as he seeks to devour all that God delights in.

There is a war on. As we begin this day, let us remember that we contend with, yes, Mammon and disease and a deeply troubled globe, but also "against the rulers, against the authorities, against the powers of this dark world and against the spiritual forces of evil in the heavenly realms" (Eph 6:12).

As we watch our spending, and watch our weight, and watch the weather forecast, are we also watching out for the devil?

Revelation 12

Yes, we must be on guard against the devil. But as we end this day, we can rejoice that his defeat is sure. As today's passage demonstrates, whatever he seeks to do will be frustrated.

He is not strong enough to attack the woman and her offspring, for she is carried away to safety. He is not strong enough to win the celestial battle, for he is hurled down by Michael and his compatriots. He is not strong enough to do what he wants to do, for he wants to defeat God and his Messiah and he simply cannot.

Heaven and earth literally war against him, and the saints he seeks to destroy eventually triumph over him. And how do they—how do we—do so?

"They triumphed over him by the blood of the Lamb and by the word of their testimony; they did not love their lives so much as to shrink from death" (v. 11).

In the face of the dragon, God calls us to trust what he has done for us, "the blood of the Lamb." In the face of the dragon, God calls us to declare this good news in "the word of [our] testimony." And, in the face of the dragon, God calls us to give our lives to his cause, even to the point of death.

If we answer that call, he will do all else that matters, and the devil will surely fall. That is the great Gift Exchange. Merry Christmas!

John G. Stackhouse, Jr.
Sangwoo Youtong Chee Professor of Theology and Culture
Regent College

Psalm 2

DAWN AFTER DARKNESS

F or those of us in the northern hemisphere, today we experience the dawn
after the longest darkness.

Some years it seems the darkness lingers. Terrible darkness. On this date
in 1988 I woke to hear that Pan-Am flight 103 had been blown out of the sky: the
famous Lockerbie bombing. The nations conspire, the peoples plot.

Psalm 2 invites us to encounter, in the midst of a moral and spiritual winter
and against the backdrop of war and injustice, one who brings peace and rules
justly: one who scoffs at the scoffer, terrifies the terrorist and rules the tyrant with
an iron rod.

Though we awake to news of misery and mayhem, we know there is one en-
throned above the nations: one to whom the most malevolent dictator will ulti-
mately have to answer. We have such confidence because God himself, one day,
opened his infant eyes for the first time within this world of darkness and death;
because he embraced that very darkness and experienced death, conquering it, in
order that we might experience light and life.

Although this is the darkest day of the year, it is also a turning.

The blazing light of the night-less New Jerusalem may be a world away from
the birth pains of a frightened teenage girl and the wailing of bereaved Bethlehem mothers; but with the Advent of Christ, the year turned. The year of the
Lord's favour began—and with each passing day we see more of his glory, and live
more in his light—the light that the darkness will never overcome.

Psalm 2

O n this date in 1995 I woke to hear that Bethlehem had passed from Israeli to Palestinian control. Was this a long-awaited liberation, a prophetic and apocalyptic sign of the end-times or a cynical political compromise? Psalm 2 reminds us that territorial boundaries and political allegiances are, at best, fluid and inconsequential. At worst, they are idols to be smashed to pieces like pottery by the

One to whom we owe our primary allegiance. No nation on earth is outside his jurisdiction.

Bethlehem has had many rulers in its day. One king in particular regarded infanticide as a justifiable national security policy. Herod had not heard of the prophecy of Micah (Mt 2:3–6); it seems he also had not read Psalm 2: "O kings be wise, be warned...serve the LORD with fear and trembling, kiss his feet..." If the empires of this world are laughable to the Most High, how much more the petty fiefdoms we create for ourselves. May we be saved from the judgment of verse 12, and instead enjoy the beatitude of his embrace: "Blessed are all who take refuge in him."

And in the corridors of power, and in the palaces of hate,
The despot and his lords conspire, this holy threat to liquidate;
Yet all the kings that e'er there were, and all the princes of this earth
With all their wealth beyond compare, could not eclipse this infant's birth.

A million monarchs since have reigned,
But vanquished now their empires vain;
Two thousand years, and still we bring
Our tributes to the Infant King. [1]

David Montgomery
Minister, Greystones Presbyterian Church, Wicklow, Ireland
Regent Alum (MDiv 1995)

---

[1] From "The Infant King" by Daithi Mac Iomaire (for the Irish tune: "The Parting Glass").

Isaiah 61:1–4

SEEING WITH HOPE

The Spirit of the Lord is upon us.

With this statement, Isaiah the prophet announced to the captives in Babylon the pending glory and restoration of Jerusalem, their beloved city. About five hundred years later, the Lord Jesus announced the fulfillment of this claim to the unbelieving city of Nazareth. In both instances, the message was clear: the time had finally come to make beautiful the broken and squalid reality of their existence. The Babylonian captives were to see the justice of God prevail on their behalf to restore Jerusalem, devastated by years of war and looting, to its former glory. The Nazarenes, disillusioned by the absence of a Messiah, were about to see the day of their own salvation.

The Spirit of the Lord is upon us today, and so we pray: May our eyes view with hope every disgruntled colleague and family member. May we see hope descend upon the anguished and desperate of our cities. May the oppressed and those who suffer injustice hear the good news entrusted to us for proclamation. May the unsung, living in squalor—who daily struggle with symptoms of addiction; whose bodies have been given over to commercial sex and abuse; who struggle to find enough to sustain themselves and their families—hear and know that Life and Salvation have come, especially for them, and for all those who believe.

All who will believe today will also be made beautiful, for the Lord has come upon us

Isaiah 61:1–4

In the course of our day we have encountered despair, cruelty, anger and destruction. We have seen many in discomfort, and some of us may be imprisoned within our own walls of exile from the Living God. Oppression and injustice have seemed to prevail over righteousness. Now evening has come, and the darkness of night enfolds us.

In spite of this, a voice cries out in the darkness, declaring unconditional love in the face of adversity: the Spirit of the Lord is here, now, and the good news is that all shall be made beautiful.

Like the captives in Babylon, this declaration allows us to live in hope, knowing that our restoration and comfort is neither limited by the many years of trouble that we have lived, nor by any unbelief. Even the vehement unbelief of the Nazarenes, to whom Jesus proclaimed these very words, could not stop the Word from being fulfilled.

The promise comes to us now with the same urgency and love with which it was first declared. The Spirit of the Lord is here with us. He comes to renew and restore all the brokenness that we continue to experience around us. We can rest in hope and peace as we wait for the final fulfillment, because we know we will rest, one day, in a city where all that was ever wretched and ruined will have far greater glory than we have ever known. A new day is coming.

Come Lord Jesus, Come.

Sophy Obuya
Bristol, UK
Education Project Officer
Send a Cow, UK
Regent Alum (MDiv 2006)

Revelation 21:1–22:5

WAITING FOR OUR FUTURE

The future, for most of us, is a blank canvas. On it we paint our dreams and then set out to translate our vision into reality through hard work and clever manipulation of circumstances. It is something we achieve.

Advent proclaims a different future—one given, not constructed. It comes to us. We do not achieve it but *faith*fully wait for it, bending our lives toward him who will come.

The season of Advent is a time of remembrance and preparation. In these Advent readings and reflections, we have already recalled and anticipated God's presence with us from creation and into the rhythm of our own lives. Now, having seen Jesus' Easter victory over Satan's draconic forces, we have begun to wait for the enthronement of God's king on Zion.

In today's passage, we see our end: a sparkling, sun-drenched, diamond-encrusted bridal city, paved with translucent gold and walled with jasper. Void of suffering and death, it is filled with glory and pulsates in an overflow of life. Its heart is the immediate, uninhibited presence of God. He has chosen to be ours, so that we may be his people from whose cheeks he will wipe away every tear of pain, mourning and death.

Since *this* future belongs to us, we can turn from every vain attempt at constructing our own future and abandon ourselves to life in the love of God.

Revelation 21:1–22:5

Waiting for the New Jerusalem on December 23, we contemplate two arrivals—the babe and the city. The expectations clash: a manger and a throne; an insignificant village and a city that covers the whole known world; a homeless child in exile and an exalted king at the centre of power; poverty, humiliation, suffering and death on the one hand, wealth, glory, abundance and life on the other.

Irreconcilable? But note who sits with the Father on the city's throne. The lamb. The defining moment in the life of the child is also the source and foundation of the coming city. Easter. The risen one who was exalted to the Father's throne is he who first died on a cross. Revelation consistently identifies Jesus as the lamb *who was slain*. It is around, through and from him that the city is shaped and held together; there would be no city to wait for, apart from the life and death of the babe in the manger.

The portrait God has painted of the future throws us back into the thick of the lives we live now. Waiting for God's presence in the coming city commences by abiding in the presence of him who was born in a manger. In the twists and turns of his journey from Bethlehem to Golgotha, we find the path to the city where water lives and leaves heal. In being conformed to his image, we are transformed into citizens worthy to serve and rule in the city of God.

Maranatha, Come, Lord Jesus, Come.

Poul F. Guttesen
Hoyvik, Faroe Islands
Part-time Minister and Sessional Lecturer
Regent Alum (MCS 1998, ThM 2000)

John 1:6–18

THE WORD MOVED INTO THE NEIGHBOURHOOD

The Word became flesh and blood,
and moved into the neighbourhood.
We saw the glory with our own eyes,
the one-of-a-kind glory,
like Father, like Son,
Generous inside and out,
true from start to finish.

John 1:14, *The Message*

When my parents left south Ukraine in the fall of 1926, they had lived through the anarchy and brutality of the Russian civil war and Bolshevik oppression. A penniless, yet thankful, family finally passed through the famous Red Gate from Russia to Latvia, then sailed from the port of Riga to Southampton, England. After a stormy Atlantic crossing on the Empress of Scotland, they docked in Quebec on October 2, 1926.

A local women's organization provided a welcome lunch and presented my mother with a copy of John's Gospel. For her, a fearful stranger in a new land, the Word had moved into the neighbourhood.

Then came the journey westward through the seemingly endless bush and rock of the Great Canadian Shield. What future could there be in such a land? A temporary residence in Winnipeg, Manitoba, meant a small house sheltering two families numbering thirteen persons.

Winter jobs for my father were scarce and paid little. The birth of my older sister, ten days after arrival in Winnipeg, brought happiness; but also, in light of an unknown future in an unknown land, apprehension. Advent and the approach of the season of joy was filled with anxiety. Mother wrote:

I was very sad that day before Christmas. During the afternoon, my husband helped the older children with their bath, then finally it was my turn. As I sat in the tub, I was overwhelmed by sadness. What a

Christmas! I could no longer hold back the tears, they ran down my cheeks and fell into the bath water. But life had to go on and I told myself I must quit this crying, so I got out of the tub and dressed. Suddenly I heard someone coming up the steps to our apartment. I opened the door a little, only to hear my husband say, "Thank you! Thank you!" I saw several ladies and a boy go down the steps and wondered what this was all about. When I came into the room I saw a large box and we began to open it. What surprises! There was a hockey stick for each of the boys as well as a puck; yes, something for each of the children; there was also a chicken, a pound of butter, some coffee and sugar. We considered all of this as a gift from the Lord.

The Word had again moved into the neighbourhood. This time in the guise of ladies from the local Anglican parish.

When God moved into the Bethlehem neighbourhood that first Christmas, he moved into a time of turmoil and tension. Our world has changed little since then. That first Christmas, there were a few in that neighbourhood who found comfort and hope in the midst of tumultuous times: a few shepherds, some kings from far off lands. Later in Christ's ministry, he touched individual lives with comfort and hope: sometimes in small villages and sometimes in large crowds outside city gates.

Maybe this is still how God moves into the neighbourhood. Quietly, without fanfare, providing for needs, storing hope for the future.

On this special night, then, the experiences of Zacchaeus, Martha, Peter, Elizabeth, Thomas and all the other individuals touched by Jesus' move into their neighbourhood, stretch to the remotest corners of the globe—ignoring race or colour. For God is still touching individual lives with hope for the future. God is still moving into the neighbourhood.

John B. Toews
Professor Emeritus of Church History and Anabaptist Studies
Regent College

Luke 2

POWER IN PRESENCE

As a young child I remember finding the first three verses of Luke 2 to be totally unrelated to the rest of the story. Why do we need to know about Caesar Augustus? Who cares that there happened to be a census throughout the entire Roman world? Who is Quirinius, the governor of Syria, and does it really matter? Knowing that everyone went to their own town to register is at least somewhat interesting, but isn't the rest of the story much more important?

Jesus is born in Bethlehem. There is no guest room available for them. It all took place in a barn. Shepherds got the first announcement. One angel speaks and many others follow. Angels' praise turns to shepherds' praise. The shepherds find Jesus in the manger, just as they were told. They tell others about the child, and go back to their flocks praising God.

That is the Christmas story.

But the gospel writer in Luke deliberately decides to root the birth of Jesus in a social and political context. Emperor Caesar Augustus issues a decree just before the ultimate potentate of all history is going to be born. A national head count occurs just before the one who knows the number of hairs on every head is about to arrive. A government act is implemented throughout the entire Roman world while the Creator of the universe makes his appearance. Quirinius is governing Syria while the Chief Shepherd becomes incarnate.

Clearly, the presence of political figures exerting their authority is all over this story. And in the middle of this show of power, a young pregnant girl and her espoused husband walk across the fields.

At the whim of a distant ruler, God incarnate, in utero, moves from one town to another. But who is following whom? The political decree set in motion by secular forces propels them on their journey, but lurking behind their steps is a much more impressive decree that will have eternal consequences. God is about to make himself present to all people, not just by a mere visit, but by incarnation—by dwelling with us. Mary and Joseph's quiet walk across the fields is a strange blend of the human and the divine.

In the context of these politicians, who have risen to positions of power and authority, arrives the servant Jesus. God dwells with us—not just as an idea, not just as a guest—but as a baby: born in simplicity, without fanfare, media attention or national adulation. He becomes present. He is here. This biblical writer, in contrast to the other accounts of the birth of Jesus, wants us to know that the Messiah was born in secular and human history. The Divine is among us in time and space.

That the one who was God would be born in such an earthy way and would presence himself with us defies human logic and elicits genuine worship.

Angels, from the realms of glory, wing your flight o'er all the earth;
Ye, who sang creation's story, now proclaim Messiah's birth:
Come and worship. Come and worship. Worship Christ, the new-born King.

Shepherds in the field abiding, watching o'er your flocks by night;
God with man is now residing. Yonder shines the infant Light:
Come and worship. Come and worship. Worship Christ, the new-born King.

Saints before the altar bending, watching long in hope and fear;
Suddenly the Lord, descending, in his temple shall appear:
Come and worship. Come and worship. Worship Christ, the new-born King.

Rod J. K. Wilson
President
Regent College

Printed in the United States
127956LV00002B/1/P